Table of Contents

This lesson plan book belongs to:

Name _____

School _____

Grade/Subject _____

Room _____

School Year _____

Address _____

Phone _____

Teacher Created Resources, Inc.
6421 Industry Way
Westminster, CA 92683
www.teachercreated.com
©2006 Teacher Created Resources, Inc.
Made in U.S.A.
ISBN 1-4206-3423-2

Managing Editor: Karen Goldfluss, M.S. Ed.
Art Production Manager: Kevin Barnes
Cover Design: Tony J. Carrillo
Imaging: James Edward Grace
Wyland® is a Trademark of
Wyland Worldwide, LLC ©2005
www.wyland.com

Teacher Created Resources

Ways to Use This Book

Seating Chart (page 3)

A seating chart is provided for easy reference. Table and desk arrangements will vary throughout the year depending on room size, available furniture, grade level taught, teaching style, and academic program needs. To accommodate a variety of classroom arrangements, you may wish to create additional charts and place specific seating information in a separate folder.

Student Roster (pages 4 and 5)

Use the roster to record information for each student. Having the roster in your lesson plan book provides you with quick and easy access to important data for both you and a substitute teacher.

Birthdays (page 6)

Use the chart on this page to write students' names and birth dates. Recognize each special day with a birthday greeting. For young children, you may wish to sing to them.

Weekly Schedule (page 7)

If your schedule changes periodically, you may wish to duplicate this page before completing your current schedule. Attach new schedules throughout the year, as the need arises.

Year At A Glance (pages 8 and 9)

Use this chart to plan units of study and/or to focus on immediate and upcoming events, conferences, meetings, seminars, and other important dates. Record each event as soon as you are notified. The Year At A Glance chart can also be reproduced for students to help them plan projects and keep track of important dates and events.

Substitute Teacher Information (pages 10 and 11)

Document all pertinent information on these pages. If you have a copy of the layout of your school, attach it to page 11. Otherwise, sketch a diagram of the school building and grounds. Be sure to show important locations, such as the office, restrooms, faculty lounge, cafeteria, auditorium, and playground.

Year-Round Activities (pages 12 – 15)

Whether you need ideas for every day, week, month, or throughout the year, the suggestions on pages 12 through 15 will help you plan ongoing activities that can be shared and enjoyed by all.

Daily quotations provide "food for thought" and help reinforce higher-level thinking skills. Quotes can be discussed in an informal setting, or students can be encouraged to write their interpretations of a quote. Suggestions and tips are provided on page 12.

Make vocabulary development part of the weekly routine by creating a priority list of words for students to learn throughout the year. The suggestions on page 13 will help you get started.

Reading and reciting poetry helps students improve a number of essential skills, including fluency. By choosing a poem each month and completing the activities on page 14, students will become more competent in the areas of oral and written communication.

The activities introduced on page 15 focus on the development of student-directed learning in a fun and interesting way. Students develop a set of "curiosity questions," research the answers, and present their findings to the class. Use the suggestions provided, or develop your own technique to help students take ownership of their learning.

Daily Lesson Plans (pages 16 – 95)

Use the Daily Lesson Plans section to help you organize your lesson plans each week. There are enough weekly plan pages to cover a 40-week school year. At the top of the left-hand page, fill in the blank to indicate the week dates for which the plans are written. The first column may be used for notes. For special programs requiring more in-depth explanation of plans, reference the specific folder, notebook, guide, etc., to which the teacher should be directed. This is especially helpful to substitute teachers.

Seating Chart

Seat Arrangement Ideas

Sticky notes can be used to temporarily assign seats.

1. Basic Row Seating

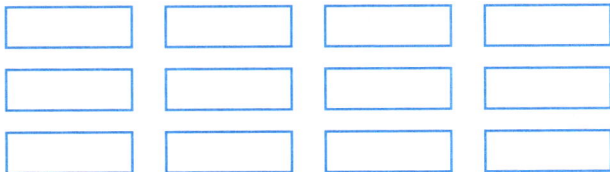

2. U-Shaped Seating

3. Rectangle Seating

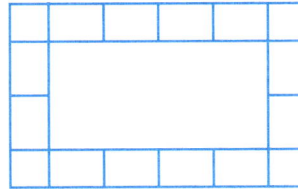

4. Partner Seating

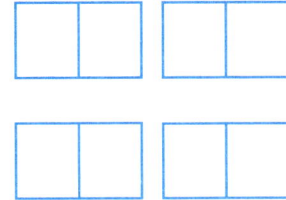

The size and shape of your room will play a large part in your seating arrangement.

You may want to change this layout once you are familiar with your students and their needs.

Regardless of your seating plan, the most important concern is that you can easily see all your students and the children in turn have good visibility of you, the chalkboard, and other focal points in the room.

Front of Classroom

Student's Name	Parent's Name	Address
1.		
2.		
3.		
4.		
5.		
6.		
7.		
8.		
9.		
10.		
11.		
12.		
13.		
14.		
15.		
16.		
17.		
18.		
19.		
20.		
21.		
22.		
23.		
24.		
25.		
26.		
27.		
28.		
29.		
30.		
31.		
32.		
33.		
34.		
35.		
36.		

Roster

Home & Work Phones	Birthday	Siblings	Notes

Birthdays

AUGUST	SEPTEMBER	OCTOBER
NOVEMBER	DECEMBER	JANUARY
FEBRUARY	MARCH	APRIL
MAY	JUNE	JULY

6

Weekly Schedule

Time	Monday	Tuesday	Wednesday	Thursday	Friday

SEPTEMBER	OCTOBER

JANUARY	FEBRUARY

MAY	JUNE

A Glance

NOVEMBER	DECEMBER

MARCH	APRIL

JULY	AUGUST

Substitute Teacher

School Schedule
- Class Begins _____
- Morning Recess _____
- Lunchtime _____
- Class Resumes _____
- Afternoon Recess _____
- Dismissal _____

Special Notes
_____
_____
_____
_____
_____
_____
_____
_____

Special Classes
Student _____

Class _____ Day _____ Time _____

Student _____

Class _____ Day _____ Time _____

Student _____

Class _____ Day _____ Time _____

Special Needs Students

Student	Needs	Time and Place
_____	_____	_____
_____	_____	_____
_____	_____	_____
_____	_____	_____
_____	_____	_____
_____	_____	_____

Where to Find
- Class List _____
- School Layout _____
- Seating Chart _____
- Attendance Record _____
- Lesson Plans _____
- Teacher Manuals _____
- First Aid Kit _____
- Emergency Information _____
- Supplementary Activities _____
- Class Supplies–paper, pencils, etc._____
- Referral forms and procedures_____
_____
_____
_____
_____
_____
_____
_____
_____
_____
_____
_____

Information

Classroom Standards

- When finished with an assignment

  _____

  _____

- When and how to speak out in class

  _____

  _____

- Incentive Program

  _____

  _____

- Discipline

  _____

  _____

- Restroom Procedure

  _____

  _____

People Who Can Help

- Teacher/Room _____

- Dependable Students _____

  _____

  _____

  _____

  _____

  _____

- Principal _____

- Secretary _____

- Custodian _____

- Counselor _____

- Nurse _____

Layout of School

Quote of the Day

Start each day with some higher-level thoughts. Quotes are clever, interesting ways to reinforce morals and values. Choose a student each day to read a quote of the day, or make it a class job to write it on the board. The student should stand in front of the class and read it two or three times aloud. Next, let the class informally pair up and discuss the meaning of the quote. The teacher may have to facilitate the process with a few lessons on literal interpretation and figurative language. *Amelia Bedelia* books are great examples of this. After the lesson, the students will understand. The teacher can also display the quote in the room for student reference.

A great quote to start off the school year is, "Every new beginning is some other beginning's end." Some other favorite quotes to use include the following:

- People may doubt what you say, but they will always believe what you do.
- You miss 100% of the shots you never take.
- Success comes before work only in the dictionary.
- The more you know, the more you know you don't know.
- You may delay, but time will not.
- A friend stands behind you when all others leave.
- Nothing is permanent but change.

✓ **Tips:**

- Write the quote on sentence strips. Laminate and place the quote in a pocket chart. As new quotes are introduced, add them to the pocket chart. As an extention, ask the class to give an example of when this quote could be useful in their lives.

- Make "Ocean Awareness" a theme throughout the year, by introducing students to the well-known quotes of acclaimed artist, Wyland. Several quotes from his book, *Wyland Ocean Wisdom* (Health Communications, Inc., 2000), are included in the daily lesson plans section of this book.

Each day and night the sea composes a symphony . . .
– Wyland

You may wish to prepare an ocean-themed bulletin board with a focus on ocean habitats and specific ways students can learn more about environmental issues and the preservation of ocean life. (A great internet source is www.wyland.com.)

Year-Round Activities

The Word of the Week

A fun way to increase your students' vocabulary and improve their writing, is to introduce a Word of the Week. Find a special spot on a bulletin board or chalkboard. Hang a creative sign announcing "The Word of the Week." Under the sign, choose a word that is useful and teaches something at the same time. Choose grade-level appropriate vocabulary. (For example, words such as *punctual, enthusiasm, independent, compassionate,* and *sympathy* are words older students can use.)

How does it work? Under the sign and the word, have an envelope with copies of the study sheet shown below. The students are responsible for learning the spelling, meaning, and part of speech for each week's word. The definition can be simple but should be based on information from a dictionary. This activity is great for reinforcing dictionary skills.

Include the Word of the Week as a bonus on a final spelling test. The word spelled correctly could be worth two points, with the correct definition worth two points, and the correct part of speech worth one point.

✓ **Tip:** Display the word on Monday and pronounce it for the entire class. Have students repeat the pronunciation. Students do the Word of the Week on Friday's spelling test from memory. Have a special location on your spelling test form to fill in the definition, circle the part of speech, and write the word. If students take their spelling test on notebook paper, it is best to include a Word of the Week form to ensure accuracy and consistency in their answers.

- -

Word of the Week

Word: _____

Part of Speech: Noun   Verb   Adjective

Definition: _____

_____

_____

_____

_____

Year-Round Activities

Poem of the Month

To introduce poems, present a poem or two each month. Choose a theme for that month and find poems to fit it. For example, January poems could be about winter. February poems could focus on friendships. Find poems that are child friendly and have an interesting rhythm.

Copy a class set of the poems, three-hole punch them, and pass them out at the beginning of each month. First, read the poem aloud, modeling the rhythm and correct pronunciation for the students.

Next, have the students read it. Splitting up the task into smaller parts focuses their attention longer, and keeps the whole class involved. For example, the girls can stand and read the first two stanzas, then the boys can stand to read the next two, and continue to alternate. There are a variety of ways to alternate the readings. Depending on the poem, the teacher may read it more than once using different groups.

The Snow-Bird
Frank Dempster Sherman

When all the ground with snow is white
The merry snow-bird comes,
And hops about with great delight
To find the scattered crumbs.

How glad he seems to get to eat
A piece of cake or bread!
He wears no shoes upon his feet,
nor hat upon his head.

But happiest is he, I know,
Because no cage with bars
Keeps him from walking on the snow
And printing it with stars.

Once it has been read, discuss the rhythm, the special wording, the description used, etc. However, there is no need to go into great detail (e.g., iambic pentameter). Remember to select free-verse poems as well.

An extension activity is to have students create a poem using similar characteristics. If the poem verses are in couplets, have them write couplet poems. If the poem uses spelling in a creative way to emphasize the poem's meaning, ask the students to do the same.

Another suggestion is to enlarge each poem to poster size. Have a volunteer color and/or decorate them to be hung in the hallway outside the classroom door. Each month the poem is taken down and given to two students, chosen at random. Once the student receives the poster-size poem, it is his or her job to read it aloud to the class one last time. Replace the poems with new ones for the next month.

✓ **Tip:** Three-hole punch the poems and have the students put them all in a poetry binder or folder. They should save the poems each month, and by the end of the school year they will have an entire collection.

Year-Round Activities

Curiosity Questions

One way to incorporate student-directed learning is through curiosity questions. To initiate this process, the teacher has the students write down a question they have about basic occurrences in life (things they have often wondered about, such as why we sneeze, why the sky is blue, or why ocean water is salty).

Students can write down on a slip of paper the following information: the date of the question, the question itself, and their name. (See sample below.) At the bottom of the paper is a line for the due date. This paper then gets stapled to the top of the notebook paper of the child who has the researched answer.

How the research works is up to the teacher. The teacher can assign each child a week to research the question and answer, or have everyone researching questions at the same time with the same due date. The teacher can have questions researched with partners or in groups. Another possibility is to have individual students create a poster about their question or use a software program to create a slide show. Five slides work well for this activity. Or, the teacher can let the class decide. Since the students created the questions, they will take interest in how to present the findings. The research should not take much time, since the questions are very specific. Students should be able to research their question in one week.

✓ **Tip:** Display the curiosity questions and a brief explanation of each on the bulletin board. Students can read each other's responses. Add a title at the top of the bulletin board, such as "Curiosity is the key to learning!"

- -

? ? ? **Curiosity Question** ? ? ?

By _____

My question is _____

_____

_____

_____

Date submitted: _____   Due date: _____

Week of _____

Monday			
Tuesday			
Wednesday			
Thursday			
Friday			

Week of _____

Monday			
Tuesday			
Wednesday			
Thursday			
Friday			

Week of _____

Monday			

Tuesday			

Wednesday			

Thursday			

Friday			

All of man's masterpieces in art can't match the living treasures in the sea...
— Wyland

Week of _____

Monday			
Tuesday			
Wednesday			
Thursday			
Friday			

– Wyland

Week of _____

Monday			
Tuesday			
Wednesday			
Thursday			
Friday			

Week of _____

Monday

Tuesday

Wednesday

Thursday

Friday

To master the oceans, we must first respect all life within…

– Wyland

Week of _____

Monday			

Tuesday			

Wednesday			

Thursday			

Friday			

Will we be the generation that cares enough to help all life on this planet?

– Wyland

Week of _____

Monday

Tuesday

Wednesday

Thursday

Friday

Week of _____

Monday

Tuesday

Wednesday

Thursday

Friday

Oceans are a place to look for inspiration...

– Wyland

Week of _____

Monday			
Tuesday			
Wednesday			
Thursday			
Friday			

The ocean delights in showing its awesome beauty to all that come to visit...
– Wyland

Week of _____

Monday

Tuesday

Wednesday

Thursday

Friday

Only in nature does one truly live…

– Wyland

Week of _____

Monday			
Tuesday			
Wednesday			
Thursday			
Friday			

Week of _____

Monday
_____
_____
_____
_____
_____
_____

Tuesday
_____
_____
_____
_____
_____
_____

Wednesday
_____
_____
_____
_____
_____
_____

Thursday
_____
_____
_____
_____
_____
_____

Friday
_____
_____
_____
_____
_____
_____

The gentle, caring nature of the whale should be adopted by man…

– Wyland

Week of _____

Monday			

Tuesday			

Wednesday			

Thursday			

Friday			

Week of _____

Monday			
Tuesday			
Wednesday			
Thursday			
Friday			

Week of _____

Monday

Tuesday

Wednesday

Thursday

Friday

The sea is an endless orchestra of light and sound...

– Wyland

Week of _____

Monday

Tuesday

Wednesday

Thursday

Friday

Week of _____

Monday			
Tuesday			
Wednesday			
Thursday			
Friday			

There, below the surface, are great forests growing from the bottom of the sea... – Wyland

Week of _____

Monday			
Tuesday			
Wednesday			
Thursday			
Friday			

Week of _____

Monday

Tuesday

Wednesday

Thursday

Friday

Once a child loves an animal they will forever defend it...

– Wyland

Week of _____

Monday

Tuesday

Wednesday

Thursday

Friday

Week of _____

Monday			

Tuesday			

Wednesday			

Thursday			

Friday			

The magic spell cast by the sea enlightens all that embrace her...

– Wyland

Week of _____

Monday

Tuesday

Wednesday

Thursday

Friday

Dolphins celebrate the true joy of living each and every day...

– Wyland

#3423 Lesson Plan Book

Week of _____

Monday

Tuesday

Wednesday

Thursday

Friday

Whales are a symbol of the wild oceans, unchanged for millions of years...

– Wyland

Week of _____

Monday

Tuesday

Wednesday

Thursday

Friday

The most insignificant ocean animal is significant to the balance of the ocean...
– Wyland

Week of _____

Monday

Tuesday

Wednesday

Thursday

Friday

No animal works harder at having fun than the dolphin…

— Wyland

Week of _____

Monday			
Tuesday			
Wednesday			
Thursday			
Friday			

Week of _____

Monday

Tuesday

Wednesday

Thursday

Friday

Week of _____

Monday			
Tuesday			
Wednesday			
Thursday			
Friday			

The sights and sounds of the sea always inspire…

– Wyland

Week of _____

Monday

Tuesday

Wednesday

Thursday

Friday

Week of _____

Monday

Tuesday

Wednesday

Thursday

Friday

Week of _____

Monday

Tuesday

Wednesday

Thursday

Friday

The world's finest wilderness lies beneath the waves...

– Wyland

Week of _____

Monday

Tuesday

Wednesday

Thursday

Friday

Each day and night the sea composes a symphony...

– Wyland

© Teacher Created Resources, Inc.

81

#3423 Lesson Plan Book

Week of _____

Monday			
Tuesday			
Wednesday			
Thursday			
Friday			

Into the ocean went a world more fantastic than any imagination could inspire... – Wyland

Week of _____

Monday

Tuesday

Wednesday

Thursday

Friday

Week of _____

Monday

Tuesday

Wednesday

Thursday

Friday

Week of _____

Monday

Tuesday

Wednesday

Thursday

Friday

Many ocean species have yet to be discovered...

– Wyland

Week of _____

Monday

Tuesday

Wednesday

Thursday

Friday

Coral reefs are the gardens of the sea, as rich and colorful as any on land...

– Wyland

Week of _____

Monday			

Tuesday			

Wednesday			

Thursday			

Friday			

The dolphin is man's best-finned friend...

– Wyland

Week of _____

Monday

Tuesday

Wednesday

Thursday

Friday

 # Notes